faceless

*For dearest Brian,
with love
Genni*

April 12/07

faceless

GENNI GUNN

John Barton, Editor

Signature

EDITIONS

Cover design by Terry Gallagher/Doowah Design.
Cover painting Smokescreen #1 (mixed media, 1999) by Ileana Springer.
Photo of Genni Gunn by John Kim.

This book was printed on Ancient Forest Friendly paper.
Printed and bound in Canada by Marquis Book Printing Inc.

We acknowledge the support of The Canada Council for the Arts and the Manitoba Arts Council for our publishing program.

Library and Archives Canada Cataloguing in Publication

Gunn, Genni, 1949–
        Faceless / Genni Gunn.

Poems.
ISBN 978-1-897109-16-8

        I. Title.

PS8563.U572F32 2007   C811'.54   C2007-901894-7

Signature Editions
P.O. Box 206, RPO Corydon, Winnipeg, Manitoba, R3M 3S7
www.signature-editions.com

for Verbena
my mother

CONTENTS

wEstSCAPES

1. wEstSCAPES

To live on the edge of a continent is to understand
the finite property of things   delicious anxiety

fear of falling   optional suicide measures — jump
into cold bluewater   submerge   float out to sea

Inland   continuity unsettles   cities rush
the thick of people   things   a constant distraction

no oceans to dream beyond   no balancing
on perilous cliffs   no hypothesis of death   Faces

stare out of windows envisioning a mountaintop
the slow   smooth glide through air   the soundless

parting of waves   Here where a continent rises
and falls possibilities for disaster are endless

an earthquake   east and west fault lines   or a tsunami
leviathan quenching its thirst in English Bay

swallowing the West End whole   or a torrent of rain
steeping the mountainside in mud   a steady flow to the sea

To balance on the outer edge is to expect paradox
equilibrium   a faint horizon between impulse and rationale

We erect amulets — THIS IS A NUCLEAR-FREE ZONE —
in the shadow of US destroyers that intermittent slice

the depths of the harbour   point to the words   hold up
banners   bob on small lifeboats in the path of steel

no more a palisade than one small man in China
waving his shopping bags to stop an army

To live on the edge of a continent is to balance
clarity of vision with an unshaken belief in myth

in semi-darkness   totems stalk us   carved eagles fly
frogs swim the water of the eye and bear claws

scratch tremors in the spine   downtown the city
face is a thin mantle crust beneath which arteries

pulse with spice and opium   cards   knife
blades   plunging into the centre of the earth

we ski in morning light and swim in afternoon
the impulse for the edge is a magnetic field

insul/isolation   and we create a story   this is our
new frontier   last chance for utopia

2. Vancouver Street

The man who follows a block at a time
curls something in his smile   His face

familiar   haunts me in the crescent
where trees cathedral a ceiling

over the street   Thick-webbed foliage
neons gold streaks and blue-star winks   His eye

licks my footsteps   heels tapping a rapid nervous
rhythm towards home   His smile

threatens from behind   His strides widen
reach mine   Backdropped by Tudor mansions

Georgian columns   Victorian facades   he grasps
a door handle to his chest — brassy   elegant —

holds it up   turns to unlatch the sky
walks past me   curves away his mangy yellow

hair ponytailed   Salvage glints like a carnival ring
beneath the Granville Bridge   his sleeping bag

under a lean-to of crates — glimpsed duck eggs
paper fans   the black maws of ships

oceans undulating and the claws of cranes   At night
a brass moon casts brilliant hues over his shoulders

the sky a corridor of doors he opens until the night
no longer crunches under his feet   until he leaves

no traces on the street   Passersby punish him
with the terrible contempt in their eyes   In the rain

the bridge glistens — a ferris wheel — tarnished steel
commuters ride home in sizzle-wet splatters

3. Like Ruins

Three weeks they prod   calibrate   x-ray
bones   muscles   gauge seismic signatures

delicate and black   like ruins
rows of stones radiating from a cairn

When I hear the word   I imagine The Tropic
of Cancer   your body stretched around

the earth   your body the earth   Mexico
Egypt   India   Saudi Arabia   China

the sun in June directly overhead
You are cutaway   in profile   an exotic terrain

faults   a sediment of sentiments   layers
of lovers   the youngest lying between

rivers   in the high plateau of the Italian Murge
the oldest leaning against Vancouver sky

You are landscape   a place to point to   YOU ARE
HERE like the red dot on a mall schematic

boxed in by lines and squares the earth suddenly flat
a constellation   a crab in the northern hemisphere

clawing the night sky   YOU ARE HERE   an X
ray irradiating fear

You push us away   take solace in your solo dance
your breast a thermal aureole   a tropic

of cancer   while we arc low in the sky
Druids used stones   surgeons a knife

rituals to spur the sun to burn
stave off light

4. Incendiaries

All summer fires rage   the forest furious
spitting ash   red embers through the air   voracious

fireflies consuming fuel oxygen heat
warnings bellow through screen doors

what does one take in an hour?
how to distil a life into an emblem or two?

After my father died my mother carried all
his possessions from house to house afraid

to choose what to let go   she carried him as well
in mother–of–pearl hinges and keys   an abalone

shell   tracked Atlantic to Pacific   buried
him nearby on a sandy beach

Grief too is a fire   its flames outrun us
burst us   spontaneous combustion   we can't

escape electrical storms churning
the wind   lightning   every which way

some relics we relinquish
others we carry around forever

To untangle a life some loot   some cry   some
videocam themselves in front of a blistering

mountain   not trusting their eyes   memory tainted
by plumes of smoke   gyre of helicopters

torrent of water   bombers overhead   we stockpile
an exquisite carved chair   an African gong

a grey cardigan leather-bound books
a letter   furtive moments of joy

In dreams   fire blows open the damper
of an old chimney and there   a nest

cassia bark   spikes of nard   cinnamon   myrrh
a firebird flies into my room   golden   red

feathers tipped in ash   a resurrection   my father
across an ocean of untold stories   I ask him all

I never asked   too young once
to imagine such loss   flames

roar   undiscerning   through memory
if we let them   their incandescence

a warning   and in this season of burning
we sift through the smouldering

ruins for a symbol to make
of our lives

5. Fossil Highway

i.

These Rockies sink to grow
return to the molten core and birth

salmon die to spawn   a plunge through rapids
battered by stumps and stone   I cannot

swim as well   bruise easily   If only I could
soar upstream on the taut strings

of a cicada wing   pluck notes thick as clouds
safety nets for a weightless fall

ii.

Watch rivers   arteries nurturing the earth
there is no need to orchestrate disturbance   Listen

water sings   birth stories spring among whirlpools
and mountains shed unwanted layers

to reveal their form   Pilgrimage to the source
The mountain speaks stone   erupts its language

from within   a furious will   without alternatives
I recognize my features in the scarred face

iii.

The river kicks disturbing echoes   spirals expand to shore
trace mother tongues in sand   If only I could read between

the grains   Language is sound the ear constructs
ambiguous as vision   hoodoo sentinels guard

an entrance   They sculpt themselves into the eye
such trickery   and what seems stone   crumbles

iv.

Currents expose the jagged edge   then reunite into
a vortex wrenching tides   I could ebb into its power

were I not heavy with memory   like salmon
landlocked   All thoughts reflected

The lake holds up a mirror of silt   lets elements resolve
the hues   In the transparency of night words runnel out

to me   ghosts seeking human form   grizzly stares
back   eye to eye   stones slide down a mountain pass

I found my name half buried in Italian earth
and still the roots cross an ocean

v.

A rainbow arches the sky   long fingers point
to an uncertain end   My hand a fossil highway

the story grows and when it hails   the blight lingers
I forge rock   threading memories   my birth tongue echoes

in the beat of wings and the eye is a shutter   sheer filigree
capturing time   elusive as bear tracks after   rain

FACELESS

FACELESS

1.

In crowds strangers jostle against her
arms and legs   In lineups people elbow

in front of her   In bars men stare
past her   She spends a quarter of her pay

on cosmetics — eye shadows   liners   blushes
foundations glows — the rainbow captive

in small compacts   And still she is

2.

Sometimes   she searches storefront windows
where mannequins stare back   eyes glazed

mouths open in surprise   arms out in supplication
She does not recognize herself inside the fiberglass

fleshtoned   flexible
fashionable   accessorized

She wears opaque layers and shades of beige
on beige   her purse a knock-off brand   her skirts and hair

too long or short   as if she were forever a step behind
running to catch a moving trend   a transformation mask

opening and closing to bewildering effect   Sometimes
she hurries past a hair salon   startled by colourful wigs

perched on smooth metallic orbs   abstract
heads   like Hun-Dun   the God of Chaos   in the legend

an implosion of orifices   a shape   a bird-like creature
other gods pitied   resolved to sculpt him features

they drilled two holes where eyes should be
a notch for nose   a rip for mouth

poor Chaos   cooped and ordered
nipped and tucked into the ideal god

sighed and died soon after
should have been warning enough

3.

She is not amorphous or chaotic   wastes time
shipshaping her apartment   arranging furniture

but no one visits   Once she was someone's wife
mothered two daughters   must have been happy too

but can't recall those details   nor the husband
who has eroded into a blur   a mound of gloom

4.

She is not faceless to her dog whose tail thumps
the moment her key pivots in the lock   his love excessive

like chocolate or the softest bed — a craving
a spike of endorphins through the veins

To her daughters   she is too boldfaced
sloe doe-eyed teens   languishing   pooled

in front of TV soaps and chat lines
where everyone is faceless

5.

A quarrel   rising counterpoint   the girls shrill
demand to the mother's martyred sobs

bickers pleas   pouts   banal exchanges   all shout
ultimatums   the girls slam into the night

thirteen   fifteen   their bodies high–risk machines
the mother calls but they don't veer

the dog barks twice then settles on the rug
the woman slumps in front of her TV

today she lost her job   her husband gone
and now her girls   she reaches in her purse

draws out the vial of pills   she'll sleep tonight
no matter what   she'll sleep and show them all

6.

Her dog is a loyal creature   He ogles her
through one slit eye

Dogs are heroic   They dive underwater
off 80-foot cliffs to save people from drowning

they climb mountains and dig for avalanche victims
one dog waited twelve years for his master

in the lobby of a hospital where he had last seen him
This woman's dog   at first   is not perturbed by her

lying on the couch   accustomed to her sluggish ruts
Reality TV   but as the hours lapse

and the woman doesn't stir   he licks her hand and face
still no response   he licks and licks her mouth and nose

his paws now claw her chin   he panics   nips at her lifeless lips
she finally hears the whine   struggles a resurrection

He saved her life   her daughters say
this dog who mauled their mother's face

7.

For months she chain-smokes on the couch
and mourns her loss — the dog put down all those

who've never seen her   shunned her or ignored her
she mourns the indifferent and the cruel

she mourns her nose   her chin   her mouth
even when all the skin has healed   jawbone exposed

one daughter gifts a puppy to encourage her outside
the other brings a dental mask to hide the faceless half

The woman ventures out   the mask a plaster cast
molding a nose   the semblance of a snout

No one gives her a second glance   this immense city noxious
with fumes   masked commuters normal as surfers in Hawaii

Inside her mask   however   she feels strange
elation   no one stares   she is still

8.

You have to wonder about spectators
Remember the minister's black veil

how an entire congregation felt he had *changed*
into something awful   only by hiding his face

Here in Paris this woman   changed and unchanged
Do neighbours wonder what sins and secrets hide

behind her mask? Their own concealed transgressions?
Does the woman smash all the mirrors

afraid to be alone with herself?
Death does not snatch the mask from her face

Death is not the mask she wears
this veil a half death   an escape

9.

What's in a face? Muscles attached to muscles or skin
The slightest contraction forms

a frown   dimples   a wink   a scowl   the rise of an eyebrow
what do they think   her family   now she can't speak or smile

now she can't smell or eat?   Beneath her mangled skin
the kissing muscle quivers   round it goes like the rubber seal

on a glass jar   it would cinch her mouth closed
pucker her lips if she had any

10.

Everyone talks about fingerprints   but really   without your face
you could be no one   Faces turn up everywhere

Presidents face the nation   heroes face adversity
we all meet face to face   lose face   put on a brave face

save face   make a face or an about-face   let's face it planets
mountains and wars have faces   fonts countries corporations

have faces   pumpkins and watches have faces
we put our best face forward   take things at face value

face-off   face up and often face the music
why even evil has a face — how in-your-face is that?

11.

What's in a skin?   Dead cells   beauty
In the BodyWorlds exhibits   cadavers

stalk the galleries   their skinless arms
bat softballs   row canoes

their skinless legs kick soccer balls and skate
their skinless hands catch basketballs

flick pucks at unseen goals
some even stand beside

themselves — skeleton and musculature
inside outside   side by side

a foot   a stocking
ready to step into their own bodies

some stare at distant points
as if embarrassed by their own disclosures

their muscle-doors hinged open
through which we glimpse the gears

the turning of our motor hearts
no wonder we don't recognize

our selves   without our skins
these restless deaths   *Sports Illustrated* musclemen

12.

The woman lives an agonizing year
half a face   her daughters tiptoe round her

everyone wears masks   then another
woman dies in a nearby town

call her Sylvia   Marilyn   Virginia
count the possible

overdoses   drownings
heads in the oven   slashes at the wrists

the hundred and hundred ways
to step out of the body

and the disfigured woman gets a second chance
new face   a transplant   a white gardenia

following afternoon sun   Or a branch
severed with a sharp clean knife

an apple grafted onto a plum
together fused   the wait

Perhaps one can't escape one's fate
The woman removes her mask

and dons a suicide face
who will she see in the mirror?

whose dead and
beating heart?

BARROOM SCENES

1. Contrails

Time   a blackbird   wings spread   the echo
of its flight   a contrail   a turbulence

of then and now   white
vapour against the blue

in humid air   back then   my other self in barrooms
underground amid the strobe of spotlights   the steady

throb of drums   the room a sewer swell   how I detested
all who mingled there with black-thorn eyes

and scale-like pelts   Tonight a wailing guitar seduces me
back into a club where   on a narrow ledge   a memory revives

I knew him when his hips were lean his eyes half
closed   I knew him when his lips could part

the thighs of women   The room is dank with sweat
and strippers' sighs   I close my eyes   He can still coax

the heartbreak from my bones   Four drinks past midnight
he strokes the rosewood neck   wipes dry the perspiration

in the curves   lays her inside the velvet case
I knew him as a careless man   his hooks strung

on silver chains   (verses   refrains)   The women
dazzled by the jeweled flies swallowed the lines

his muscles rippled   reeled in the catch   he laughed
I knew him when he wrenched out hooks and left

an open gash   We speak a bit of when I shared
his stage   condoned with silence what I could

now avenge   but it's too late   his forehead high
his pupils tight in a grey face I do not recognize

Instead I sit and listen   his fingers pluck the years
and we cross a mountain range   clouds fall

into the yellow tail of summer
vermillion trails of longing we followed

2. Stripped

She steps into the glare   small talk and bass drum
beats   Anonymous woman imprisoned in the stare

of lonely men who live only through their eyes
her breasts an idea of happiness — like watching

TV in solitude   like watching a Chinese girl   unravel
her tiny feet bound into servitude   the flesh deformed

into an idea of beauty   (and the men shout *take it off*)
While in the room next door   I'm up on stage

guitar strapped on like a shield — another woman
another life unfolding in front of men who crowd

in bars and roar   morning-glory men   large showy
faces purple blue pink   their hands squeeze the necks

of bottles   their chests swell with primal screams
raised in almost any soil   they run wild   choke

everything with heart-shaped leaves   *parasite plants*
flowers lasting only hours   I fear the communal howl

biceps flexed   heads swinging   to the rhythm
of my fingers plucking strings   to the rhythm

of my voice (and the men shout
take it off)   strangers I both recognize

and don't   these lovers and husbands whose private loves
are heartbreaking and fragrant as fresh white blooms

3. At the Piano Bar

I've been programmed   *smile*   no matter what
man sits at the piano bar   lip-synching to my mouth

my fingers   tunes forgotten by his heart   these strings
between us   taut nerves   struck wires   melodies glide on

slide into him   veins bulge   his Adam's apple bobs
he fumbles in his pocket   drops fivers in my brandy glass

crisp aqua watermarks   *Play me a love song* he whispers
much too near   I've been programmed   *listen*

the grating click   nails slapping keys slapping the face
that leers over the rim   "What are you doing here?"

a question he should ask himself   I poker-smile his
hands into his pocket   loosen the knot of bills

and he unravels the familiar ties   a wife somewhere
an empty suite upstairs   too many trips this year

a mine   an oil well   head office in New York   he is
always better   more   a President   a Partner   a Capital

Letter   no ordinary man ever sits across
from me   I've been preprogrammed   *hail*

these moguls made of air   The waitress ghosts
to his side   tray balanced   silent as programmed as I

a nod   an eyebrow raised   another round   he marvels
at her memory   so many suits   linens wools silks

no polyesters here   stems and rims   four   five to a table —
she has remembered his   I smile at her   behind the bar

each table lettered   each seat numbered   each drink
entered   deleted   entered   deleted   twelve hours

a day   six days a week   These strings tense between us
form a grid   and men pencil themselves in

4. Barroom Scene

How easy to forget   recall only sex and stalking
a silhouette roving amid tables sticky and wet

growling   for rounds of draft   candles glowing
pushed-up breasts   pickup lines fresh and bland

wine and Gitanes on a stranger's tongue   The barroom
bloats with laughter   from between lips a stiletto melody

carves moments in time   quills rise   imbed
themselves in open wounds   Women check motherhood

at the door   tags lost amid sculptures in the floor
engraved by spurs   spikes   music's steady crescendo

I once had a pair of dancing shoes   my pores alive
underfoot   across the city wherever there is still

darkness and sweat and bodies trying to lose them
selves   I am among the velvet flowers on the walls

embossed in a shade of dried blood   I am the features
of a woman woven in paper   the stale perfume

and pollen   the ground bass   and fine white dust
the needle-studded veins   the indelible damage

FLORENCE

FLORENCE

1.

Most families have one   a cousin or an aunt
a sister   perhaps   who flutters at the edge of family

reunions   (notice it's always a woman)   Distant
seen/unseen   frightening/benign   strange/familiar

in the mirror of our eyes   or in the liquid quivers at the edge
of laughter   Three cardigans in summer   open-toed sandals

in a downpour   floppy straw hat yanked over an ear
brown paper bag clutched like a newborn to her breast

She might paper her walls with *The Pope Buys Back Souls
from Satan* or *Space Aliens Inject Their DNA in Unsuspecting Boy* —

with the five subscriptions that slam each month against her door
She might stretch her pension along a soup-line

adopt children overseas   fill drawers
with blue parchment drawings

We avert our eyes as if she were naked   pat her arm
nod   curl condescending smiles   Later   an uncle

or a nephew drives her home   the rest dissect her
wondering how or why she left herself behind

2.

She was not always like this   Look —
in the black-and-white photo   the pretty girl stares

into the camera's eye   She is nineteen   her future
a happily-ever-after   her alabaster cheeks glisten in the flash

her lips a crescent moon   Outside the frame
uniformed men and women watch   heads cocked

small frowns of wonder — who can resist her
pinched waist   mid-calf skirts   platform shoes

dancing in officers' mess halls
her submarineman husband tall and lanky at her side

How does unease take hold in the brain?
Does it blossom   an orchid   a white ghost   elusive

or creep like a bramble
torn flesh and bruised lips?

3.

In her middle years   Florence — that is her name —
was a museum of fears mounting   her life a

macular degeneration — its centre   a black hole   the outside
a fleeting circle spinning ever faster   out of her control

Inside her house   tabloids and TV now blare disaster
after disaster as if listing the missing in action

    Giant Earthworms Terrorizing Nevada!
disease   dysfunction   disturbing high-tech malfunctions

    SARS Comes From Mars!
government corruption   child seductions

    US Paying Space Aliens to Find and Destroy Osama!
murders and burglars

    Oldster Beaten With His Own Leg During Robbery!
the self-possessed and the dispossessed

    My Husband Thinks He's a Klingon!
who might   at this moment   be hovering outside her door

4.

(Her TV screen explodes with foreign countries
multiple images   identical   burned-out

children sobbing   stomachs bloated   old man or woman
frowning in a doorway   peasant clothes   bloodied arms

anachronisms in what looks like a modern film set
Hollywood North   soldiers spiffed out

in front of the courthouse   machine guns
rounds of ammunition wound across their chests

their green camouflage gear stark against the grey of sky
and skyscrapers   against their grey asphalt hearts)

5.

No wonder she adds locks to her doors   bolts   sliders
combinations   turns off the phone   shuts the blinds

the outside world turns filthy in her eyes
she buys detergents   bleach   buckets and mops

empties the rooms   one by one   scrubs and scrubs
until her hands are bloodied too   her arms raw and weeping

this is how the world closes in   a bit at a time
so gradual no one notices   least of all oneself

6.

Seattle   December 2001   she has given
my husband strict song-lyric instructions

knock three times / step off the porch
stand on the sidewalk in front of the house

until she can determine who we are
and even when we step inside — blinds down

curtains drawn in perpetual night — her husband
peers at us   be-wild-ered   asks if we are who we say we are

We are here   we say   *we are us*
I was expecting eccentric octogenarians

magazine cut-outs in gaudy hats   who own dozens of cats
garden gnomes and pink flamingos   build egg-carton sheds

I'm not prepared for them raw-boned   skins sallow
joints jutting at every angle   her hands   fluttery

his lack of memory   She is elfin
in green rubber boots   blue cashmere coat

face joyful behind cat's-eye glasses bought in her teens
lips parted around four teeth — fangs in a Cheshire smile

7.

Near deaf   near blind   near no one
she won't answer the phone   turn on the stove

plug in the fridge   the washing machine
the dryer   anything mechanical or wired

(later   she'll play with our car's automatic window
up and down   up and down   *Oh!* she'll say   *Oh!*)

I extend my arm and she steps back
     don't touch

anything   *don't move*
anything   *don't*   *don't*   *don't put*

anything
where it's not supposed to be   *don't touch*

                                                        me

8.

It's nerve-wracking being here
both of us spooked

I might inadvertently   blunder
into a *Twilight Zone* rerun

where each false step detonates a bomb
in a faraway town   or stumble

on thick carpets of black dust
against the floor registers

that turn to soot or tumble
into her maze of large brown paper bags

rows upon rows through which she
navigates words and more words —

newspapers   bills   flyers   the fearful
stench of letters and medicines

pushed to the bottom   or fumble
in the closet and disturb her blue Jackie O suit

shoulders topped by a residue of dust
like snow fallen placid over memory

above us   the ceiling paper hangs in strips
as if to lick us with green mouldy tongues

9.

Brown paper   blue envelopes   white plastic sacs
grey dust   umber couch   black-and-white TV

brown-madder window shades   burnt-sienna curtains
oak-floor planks on which she paces

in her indigo coat and violet socks
peering into bags where multi-hued tabloids shout

that aliens are *tap tap tap*
                              ping
into her brain *tap tap tap*
                              ping

into her   wide   open eyes
that dart from left to right

she shuts the door   shuts the windows
shuts out shouts out   the tornado

in her chest   in her hands trembling
cupped in prayer to God Glob Globe

please cover the lights the glares of life
like stilettos through her eyes

10.

Where were her sisters and brothers
their husbands and wives   her nieces and nephews

where were they when she was like you and me
before her thin thin legs danced in an empty house

before her thin thin arms sealed up windows and doors
and mouths   the cupboards gaping gasping air

thick with the stench of bleach leeching into the pores
fingers pumice-raw with toxins   all those *National*

Enquirers   poisons   screaming from the inside
of big brown bags where she stores all the words

she cuts out the threats
the hocus-pocus locusts

underlines all the mines and fines
the suspicious religious ambitious

the brands and scams   her ink-black hands waving
manic   panic birds in a silent violet night

And I am speechless   paralyzed by the impossible
I close my eyes and think of the other Florence

David   Dante   Giotto's crucifix
the past spacious with statues of saints and martyrs

eternally virtuous eternally selfless
the city's cerulean eyes fixed on a distant horizon

SINGLE

1. Impersonator

Dress up like the person you were at nineteen
or thirty   fall in love with your own image

see that it is only water   Or sit on a piano stool
Liberace at the Imperial Palace and waterfall

the keyboard   hands curled into plump grey mice
Don't forget the garnets   zirconia   quartz

the pompadour   rouged cheeks
faux smile a monument to sentiment

Or step inside a skyscraper   discover
a permanent exhibit   NATURE —

ONE FLOOR UP   Stuffed gulls screech
against a celluloid sea   ripples in the sand

are real   the crash of waves hypnotic   unnerving
Photoshop the person you'd like to be

impersonate yourself   cheer and applaud
the impossible   the scent of bark

flutter of wings   chiaroscuro of a digital sun
your eyes an HDTV   memory flickering

fall in love with the you
in you   remember the water

2. Voyages

i.

Some chase it with money (love's glossy
perfection   a tourist brochure)

fly around the world and discover
nothing of their own geography

ii.

Some stay in bed   afraid the early bird
always snags the worm (don't be deceived

worms come in all shapes and sizes)
a nine-to-five job   a bus to work

the first snowflake (cold and insubstantial)
or simply the fear of rediscovering

an old lover wriggling up through a lawn
of denials   of forgetting that some worms thrive

on separation (often it's hard to tell which is the head
which is the tail) they double   multiply (serial

monogamies) and keep returning new
faces (familiar)   same centipede demands

iii.

Some let their fingers drive them into a netscape
velvet videolove   soundless / faceless

interpassive dates   where travellers unravel
highspeed lies in search of each other

(if only they could study it at school   anima / animus
tall dark and handsome / blonde slender beautiful

embed chips in their hands   like roadmaps
and always arrive on time   refreshed)

some journey into deserts wearing the prickly skins
and cactus eyes of one-night stands and *I do's*

princesses seek toads seek princesses
all for a kiss of awakening

3. Animations

Not so different from what happens
in middle years   you fall in love   again

stupidly   like the first time   only you're afraid
to let yourself be drawn in   frame by frame

remembering your past   imperfect   tracings
of a lover's pencil   how his animation

created static movements   your hair
a spider's web   your mouth a Venus flytrap

and he always the fly   and when you said
I love you   he sketched a hand in farewell

perhaps it's better left to computer morphing
less margin for error   just key in first meeting

and render the final kiss   embrace
the random graphics in between

4. Bear

A woman fell in love with a bear   Not a spirit
a black or a polar bear   not an Ursa Major

or Minor (although she was the type of woman
who could fixate on a star and later discover

it was a satellite)   He was a man-bear   coarse
stubble and heart   a man-bear who growls

and gruffs at strangers and friends and lovers
for no observable reason   who turns on you

when you meet him on a nocturnal path
haunches grizzled   claws out   solitary man-bear

who wears red-flannel shirts and dirty blue jeans
who'd rather sit on a log and sharpen his ax

than go to Starbucks and a movie   who hibernates
in Mexico all winter   and when he does return

in spring or summer   he may or may not call
the woman who has loved him in absentia

he may or may not let her into his den
which is why the woman has waited   waits

will always wait   love camouflaged   in the rifle-
butt against her shoulder   in her eyes unwavering

5. Schiavo

Something eating her
or eating at her   carving

her from the inside
and outside — a sculpture   honed

bones jutting out of her clothes like badly
hidden shoplifted merchandise

How she survived so long   her stomach
an eggshell blown empty   her smile

pumpkin-knifed   her exterior brittle
while her husband watched and her mother

watched and her father watched
and her friends watched and she watched

them all watch her watch them
as she ate away at herself

until she split apart   cardiac arrest
as if her heart had broken a law

as if her heart had broken   her brain shucked
and she   a walnut husk on the kitchen floor

and later the seasons in vacant sleep-
wake   absent even from herself

for fifteen years her parents clothed her
clothed her husband in lawsuits and briefs

when all he wanted was a shroud
to wrap her in   they fed their daughter

one drop at a time   a woman who could
not swallow   the thought of food

Schiavo
the Italian word for *slave*

6. In the Absence of Poems

The woman had a stroke and imagined
herself a poet   so she asked me to write

a preface for her imaginary book
reached out both hands as if to place

a manuscript in mine   Her hands of course
were empty   and this emptiness weighed

but I said   of course   and turned the pages
of air   imagined poems she might have

written   based on what her daughter told me
in the voice daughters have for their mothers

based on what her husband whispered   *bully*
overbearing   strict   cold   but when I pared

their words away   I found a woman chained
to her own heart   who imagined herself free

In the absence of poems we sat all afternoon
our hands entwined   the air fragrant   heavy

7. Single Mothers

for Debbie

i.

Single mothers are common as myths   spin surrogate-father lies
their children are forced to believe   Take for example Clymene

who sits by the side of a river and tells her son that his father
rides the chariot of sun   a duty as essential as her mother role

You could be anyone   the woman next door on social assistance
Each year another child   another father to invent — romantic excuses

for each wandering man   who could be Apollo straddling a fiery
throne   distracted by a circle of seasons   until his son Phaeton

looms in the lozenge of a tavern doorway watching a mouth
hunger the dawn and dusk of bottle and bottle   wondering

about the man who squats in front of the liquor store
guitar slung over his chest   his fingers strumming strings

his lips mouthing old tunes   sad songs   his hat
upended in the dust as if this were the scene

of a shootout at the OK Corral   the tassled arms   the rawhide
jacket worn and creased   the jeans   the threadbare knees

ii.

Mythical fathers acknowledge grown sons   fathers who are
gods and male and exempted from alimony   Besides

now the weaning's done and they need not concern
themselves with diapers and sleepless nights

Your womb has been a dark rotating door   welcoming faceless
fathers into a night of stars   a milky way streaming

onto your thighs   Your son begs proof of paternity — *Apollo*
you say   His father welcomes Phaeton into a sky without women

except for Aurora who's necessary for parting the gates
which she does faithfully each morning like a mistress

renouncing a lover   You're now forgotten   a moon
eclipsed by a brilliant sun   and this occurring

eons before blood tests and DNA   Apollo grants him a wish
At dawn you rise to the stale odour of a physical sensation

worn off much like the beer   Only a headache remains
dull and persistent as the mutter of babies awakening

iii.

Of course   there will always be mad reversals   gender
benders   maternities   paternities   lawsuits

and breaches   You could be   for example   that pregnant
woman who refuses a wedding ring *because he doesn't love me*

The mythical father proves his devotion by slapping
an eviction notice into your hand   then at the baby's

birth   he slaps a writ on your bed for breaching
the contract (you failed to practice birth control) as if

it were a sport   fraud (you lied about the pill)   and conversion (no
not religious) for *intentionally acquiring and misusing* his sperm

without his consent   Imagine your son a teenager one day
reading these quotes from his parents' mouths

the sperm a gift you say *transferred to me voluntarily*
a kiss   a plush armadillo   chocolates champagne genetic

bliss   That you did not *intentionally acquire it
to misuse it*   How romantic is that?

iv.

Your son drowns in the swelter of sheets in the ebony
weight of footsteps dwindling to the drip of a tap

Phaeton   ungrateful   chooses to ride the sun round the earth
What good is your mother-role now?   Your son hugs disaster

Apollo hands him the reins with a shrug
He's heard of adolescence from reputable sources

Your son swears at all his mythical fathers and dreams
a wafer of sun devouring the squalor   Phaeton rides

the curvature of Earth   blossoms open their eyes
dewdrops sigh into soil   Of course it's all too easy

Phaeton snaps the whip   urges the horses faster   closer —
as expected of a young man's first unbridled conceit

A ray trails the earth like a flyaway hair   scorches horizons
You pull off his sheets   Phaeton lets go of the reins   Icecaps form

Apollo covers his eyes   shrugs again   orders lunch   and swears
off mortal women who cannot raise responsible sons

V.

Perhaps your pitiful cries rouse Jupiter who props up
on elbows to watch the display   he's angry   after all

if the sun is so erratic   who will take his thunderbolts
seriously?   He yawns   hurls a zigzag   Phaeton explodes

Apollo orders dessert   grumbles how troublesome illegitimate
sons are   dumb as Icarus   wings crumpling into torrid sky

So much for mythical fathers
So much for mythical sons

vi.

He leaves home one morning   on the second day
of the month   before dawn   the rent in his breast pocket

Clymene still sits by the river   a poplar shedding amber tears
You peer through the slit in the curtains at the slow gait

of your son's leaving   dull and persistent
as the mutter of babies awakening

HANDS

HANDS

1.

Long-fingered   short   squat hands   elegant   baby
piggy hands   bejeweled hands   the white hands of bakers

the tarred hands of roofers   the scarred hands of carpenters
the pin-pricked hands of seamstresses   cold   warm   icy   hot hands

the first thing he notices in women   His mother's coaxed him
to sleep   stroked his face   forehead to chin   her fat   warm fingers

pillowed over his eyes   Later   chocolates   seashells curved in her fist
Her hands wrapped tacos   pounded dough   waved from doorways

pointed to distant cities on a map   licked back his hair
smoothed wrinkles from his clothes   Her hands shook kisses

from the ends of her fingers   the ones bound at death
by a rosary   palm against palm   over her breast

2.

He owns a tortilla plant at the heart of a Mexican village —
a cruciform of windowless rooms with metal door-fronts

that roll up and down morning   noon and night ·
His wife Ambida ambles at his side   her bracelets dangling

jangling   her hands submerged in flour oil and water
White fingers feed a flotilla of dough

into the silver tortilla machine that rustles and bustles
with pulleys and belts and separates dough into small balls

drops them onto conveyers and sprayers
where they are pressed into flat imperfect circles —

coiled serpents — and eased into ovens   Ambida is vain
and beautiful   has exquisite hands   She's careless

one day   while she stares at her silver reflection
her bracelet catches the edge of a lever   She feels

the wrench   the drag   She screams and screams
her husband rushes in but it's too late

At the hospital   they amputate her right hand
Does this mean she will never have a second-in-command?

Can one have a right-hand man without a
(   )

longing   a missing limb   an ancestor
beauty   an empty bed   memory

3.

This story is true   It happened more or less
like this in a small Mexican village where retired

Canadians escape to in winter   their humongous
motor homes semi-circled like wagons in the old west —

a garrison facing the sea   I say 'more or less'
because much of what we know has already

happened   in some form or other
or is happening now   or will happen

4.

In the archetypal fairytale   a man is tricked by the Devil
into trading his daughter for a sack of gold

(Insert here other treasures worth a daughter
Insert here your own story   Remember the hands

are used as metonymy   Example: *the sword* for *military power*
In schizophrenia   metonymy is a disturbance of language)

The girl   however is so pure that the Devil cannot touch her
Take away her water he commands   *Cut off her hands*

and the father chops them off   The girl weeps
her tears washing her clean   The Devil retreats

The father beams at the girl   his arms open   *you're safe*
as if   as if

She flees into the forest   a handless beast
starving   unable to feed herself

If forced to confess   the father would say
he'd consumed the sack of gold   He'd say

The Devil made me do it
How often have we heard that?

5.

Lupe comes to work for the man and his wife
She is seventeen and as fierce and wild as her name

Oh she has beautiful hands the man thinks
Long thin white fingers with rounded nails

half moons and solar eclipses   When she waves her hands
he sees butterflies fluttering in spring   When she wraps tortillas

her fingers are hummingbirds   Inside his head
her hands conduct an orchestra   perform piano concertos

pluck the strings of a harp
depress the keys of a piccolo

6.

You've got to hand it to him
Two women in the same plant

this wife and wolf-girl   a + b = c
a = Ambida b = Lupe and c = the man

who stupidly believes himself the sum
of the two women   Their three

hands *his*   A three-legged stool
trinity   the webbed feet of a duck

7.

Weeks pass months   Lupe's hands
rove inside the man's shirt

and pants   Her fingers are tongues
and teeth and mouth   Watch them lip-synch

8.

Ambida learns to use her left hand
She's both in good and bad company

Joan of Arc was left-handed   as were Jack
the Ripper   the Boston strangler   She manages

poorly   aware of her husband's rambling
hands   of Lupe's swelling

abdomen   Ambida too has children
in tandem   They are all born with two hands

9.

(The following common tools require left-to-right wrist
turning movements   making it difficult for left-handers

corkscrew   rotary-dial phone   analog clock-setting
winding   lightbulbs   screws   The following are

designed for right-handers   scissors   can openers
coffee makers   computer keyboards   calculators

pushbutton phones   golf clubs   musical instruments
cars built in right-lane countries   most handheld tools

industrial meat slicers   drill presses   band saws
textile machines   production lines   heavy equipment)

10.

The Canadian women come from the trailer park
They've been watching this drama unfold for years

during the winter months they spend in Mexico
They sit in the front pew   in pastel polyester pants

topped by shapeless shirts in tropical prints
the flowers large and sprawling

wild undergrowth lodged
in the women's soft fleshy folds

Lupe's sisters and mother and friends are unafraid
of desire (this is a baptism after all not a death)

Their skirts and sweaters hug their curves
expose thighs and half-moon bays

We are all sinners the priest says   fingers touch
forehead heart   left shoulder   right

as if he were giving erratic directions
The faithful follow   their hands a crossing

Thick shoulders droop under guilt's weight
Anxious hands cover a smile

wave away love
keep joy coiled tight in a fist

Hands absolve   pound mattresses and knead dough
strangle and stab   draw and sculpt   break and set bones

clap and slap   comb hair make maps   shoot arrows
and tend fires   they grasp and pull us   together   apart

11.

In the Inuit's Sedna legend   in a storm   the father
throws his daughter overboard to save himself

She clings to his skin boat   fingers clamped round the edge
Her body grips and grasps and torques   until her father

turns and chops her fingers off   She watches them trail through
water   reborn as   fish and seals   walruses and whales

as she too trails through fathoms   sinks to the ocean
floor   a mighty spirit   dead   (Notice that nothing

haunts her father — *An eye for an eye* my eye
should read *a hand for a hand* —

one quarter of the brain's motor cortex
powers the muscles of both hands)

12.

Ambida visits the blacksmith and brings
specifications — the hand contains

29 major and minor bones
29 major joints   123 ligaments

17 muscles in the palm   48 nerves   30 arteries
and nearly as many smaller branches

She asks him to forge her a silver hand
(different from a golden handshake)

He casts a glove   intricately carved   a re-creation
of the void   into a filigree

of beauty   Each joint moves
and when she forms a fist

her fingertips curve through a spiral —
the lengths of the finger bones equal

to the ratio of the Fibonacci numbers 2 3 5 8
Ambida wears her new hand

like a wedding band
Her husband shudders at its cool touch

13.

They might have carried on like this forever
Lupe in a new apartment   three children now and the husband

who stays two days a week   Ambida trying to manipulate
her metal hand and his heart   But one day while staring

into the silver tortilla machine   Lupe feels
the wrench   the drag   She screams and screams

the husband rushes in   but it's too late
Afterwards   at the hospital   they amputate her left hand

14.

The girl in the fairytale undergoes a series of trials
near-starvation in the woods   a marriage to a prince

a pair of silver hands   a wicked stepmother   deceit
and imbroglio   finally a banishment to the original forest

where   when she manifests a moment of selfless
devotion   her hands are magically restored

15.

Not so for Ambida or Lupe who still live
in a small Mexican village

no golden arms or silver handshakes
no exhilarating epiphanies   no hands restored

not even a prince   Lupe sits in a chair and stares
straight ahead   her children tug at her skirts

crying   hungry   tired and thirsty
No matter how long she weeps   the tears

do no more than stain her shirt
and ring her eyes in red

The Canadian women visit often   their faces
bright with pity   Ambida visits too

as does her husband
who is strangely calm

Muscles power the fingers   are strong
enough to bear the body's weight

by the fingertips   Think of those
movies where the hero dangles

from a cliff-face   Think of this
man in Mexico   Think a + b = c

ACKNOWLEDGEMENTS

Some of these poems have appeared in different forms in
Contemporary Verse 2, The New Quarterly and *Quarry.*

I would like to acknowledge all the people who appear in various
disguises throughout this collection, strangers and friends and loved
ones, being themselves or my perception of them. They shall all
remain nameless, if not faceless, except for Florence.

Thank you to the Banff Centre for giving me the opportunity to
work uninterrupted, and to the staff for their generosity and
hospitality while I was resident there; and to my agent, Carolyn
Swayze, for her continued friendship and support.

My thanks and appreciation to Carolyn Smart, Patrick Friesen, and
Diane Watson for reading drafts of these poems as they unfolded.
And a special thanks to John Barton for sharing my head space
during our slow (and sometimes quick) email game of ping-pong,
for his sharp attention to detail, and for playing by ear. And of
course, endless gratitude to Frank for absolutely everything.

ALSO BY GENNI GUNN

POETRY

Mating in Captivity

NOVELS

Thrice Upon a Time
Tracing Iris

STORIES

On The Road
Hungers

OPERA LIBRETTO

Alternate Visions

POETRY TRANSLATIONS

Devour Me Too by Dacia Maraini
Traveling in the Gait of a Fox by Dacia Maraini